THE MAKING OF A PICTURE BOOK

WRITTEN BY RODNEY MARTIN
ILLUSTRATED BY JOHN SIOW

Gareth Stevens Children's Books
MILWAUKEE

This is the story of a picture book called There's a Dinosaur in the Park! *It all began with something every story needs — an idea.*

For Jude

For a free color catalog describing Gareth Stevens' list of high-quality children's books call 1-800-433-0942

The publisher wishes to thank the following people and companies for their valuable assistance in the production of this book — for photographs: Paul Martin 5, 16; Matthew Groshek 8, 22; Kate Kriege 17, 21 (inset), 23; Dan Hoffman 24 (bottom), 25, 27, 28, 29, 30; Ken Novak cover, 20, 21, 24 (insets), 26, 27 (inset), 28 (inset), 29 (inset), 30 (inset and case); — and for permission to photograph their premises: National Colorite Corporation, Milwaukee, Wisconsin, and Worzalla Publishing Company, Stevens Point, Wisconsin.

Library of Congress Cataloging-in-Publication Data
Martin, Rodney
    The making of a picture book.

    "First published in South Australia by Era Publications"—T.p. verso.
    Summary: The author relates in text and illustrations how he came to create a picture book about a dinosaur.
    1. Picture books for children — Juvenile literature. 2. Children's stories — Authorship — Juvenile literature. [1. Picture books. 2. Authorship] I. Siow, John, ill. II. Title.
Z1037.A1M376   1988   808.06'83   88-42911
ISBN 1-55532-958-6

North American edition first published in 1989 by

Gareth Stevens Children's Books
RiverCenter Building, Suite 201
1555 North RiverCenter Drive
Milwaukee, Wisconsin 53212

First conceived, designed, produced, and published in Australia by Era Publications as *The Story of a Picture Book*, by Rodney D. Martin, with an original text copyright © 1981 by Rodney D. Martin.

US edition copyright © 1989 by Gareth Stevens Inc.

Design, US: Kate Kriege
Editor, US: Rhoda Irene Sherwood

Printed in the United States of America

3 4 5 6 7 8 94 93 92 91 90

TABLE OF CONTENTS

THE AUTHOR

The author was relaxing at home one day, when his three-year-old son ran in from a nearby park.

"I saw a dinosaur in the park!" shouted the son excitedly. "He lives under the trees. He had fierce eyes and sharp teeth. I threw a drink can into his mouth and he ate it. He eats anything. I ran away but he didn't chase me."

As his son wandered off to do something else, the author thought, "What an unusual thing to find in a park. It sounds like a good idea for a story." So before he forgot about it, he went to his desk and quickly wrote down what his son had said.

I SAW A DINOSAUR IN THE PARK
He lives ~~among finally~~ the trees
He had ~~ts~~ fierce round eyes

He had long sharp teeth

I threw a drink can into his mouth. He ate it. He eats anything.
I ran away but he didn't chase me.

Then he placed his note in a file marked IDEAS. It stayed there with several other IDEAS notes for nearly two years.

The author was not aware that he was thinking about the story at all. But all that time the idea must have been lurking deep in his mind. For one day, when the author was driving near the city, he saw this scene.

Immediately, the author felt that he had solved a problem. "I've got it!" he thought. "An idea for the dinosaur story." He had a picture in his mind of what the book would look like and what would happen in the story.

The author then had to write the manuscript. The word "manuscript" is from two old Latin words meaning "written by hand." This was the author's first attempt at writing the story.

The author's first draft of the story.

But these words did not seem right. So he wrote the story again.

Hey! I saw a dinosaur in the park.

He lives in the trees and bushes.

He's had got fierce round eyes

and long sharp teeth and spikes on his back.

I threw an old drink can into his mouth.

He ate it. So I gave him some paper

and tins and boxes and he ate them too.

I touched his spikes.

He didn't bite me. So I jumped on his tail and walked up his back and had a ride on him. He let me.

Hey! There's a dinosaur in the park.

I saw him. He lives in the bushes.

He's got fierce eyes and a ~~mean~~ mouth with sharp ~~dagger~~ teeth

and (spikes) sticking out on his back. He's ~~to~~ scary.

Hey! I saw a dinosaur in the park. He lives in the

The author's second draft.

These words did not seem right either, so he added some words and changed others. Sometimes he spent hours just thinking and not writing at all. Some days he would rewrite the whole story. Some days he would just change a word or two, until . . .

Hey! There's a dinosaur in the park.

I've seen ~~saw~~ him. He lives in the bushes where it's dark.

He's got ~~fierce horrible~~ ~~fierce round~~ eyes (and a ~~mean~~ ~~big~~ mouth

with ~~long~~ sharp dagger teeth) and ~~spikes~~ spikes sticking out on his back.

~~He's SCARY.~~

Hey! I saw a dinosaur in the park. crunching

He's got a dangerous tail and a jaw full of sharp teeth

I threw an old drink can into his mouth

A sample of the author's working notes.

. . . the manuscript became messy. In fact it became so untidy that the author could hardly read his own writing.

After the story had been written and changed many times, it gradually began to say what the author felt was right.

7

An author's manuscripts often become so untidy and difficult to read that they must be typed. So the author had to type his manuscript using his word processor.

During the typing, the author once again changed some details because he was not quite satisfied with his writing. And he knew that this would not be the last time he would alter the words of the story.

The author typed his manuscript.

There's a Dinosaur in the Park!

Hey! There's a dinosaur in the park!

I've seen him. He lives in the bushes where it's dark.

He's got fierce eyes and sharp dagger claws
and sticking-out spikes all down his back.
He's SCARY.

He's got a dangerous tail
and a giant jaw full of crunching teeth.

He was hungry, so I threw an old drink can into his mouth.

He ate it. So I gave him some paper and tins and boxes and things
HING.

his tail and up his back
mped his sharp dagger claws
ent "RRR-R-A-A-AAH!"

t him.

yed in the park.

I might see that dinosaur again tomorrow.

In picture books, words do not tell all the story. The pictures tell a lot. So the author began to plan what the pictures might show. He described each picture. He invented characters, scenes, and actions that would not be described through the words. The author had to see these things in his mind.

He had to think about what the characters would look like and what they would be doing and thinking. All these things would not be mentioned in the text, the words. In fact, on some pages there was to be no text at all.

He described each picture beside the words to be printed with it. This is what he wrote about the first picture.

The author's notes for illustrations.

Hey! There's a dinosaur in the park.

Ben is a four year old boy. He is a rather casual looking child, slightly scruffy, dressed in jeans, sneakers and T-shirt with some kind of favorite character printed on the front.

Ben looks as though he has been playing in the park, pictured in the background. He is speaking to a boy some two or three years older than he. Ben is excited, displaying a feeling of personal urgency in trying to convince the older boy that there really is a dinosaur in the park. He (Ben) is bearing the world's most exciting news at that moment.

The older boy considers the young lad to be beneath him — he has the air of superiority that comes with being two or three years older. The boy is idly tying his shoelace, trying not to pay too much attention to Ben but obviously gaining some personal ego boost from being able to see how "juvenile" the younger boy is compared to him — therefore he at least has to acknowledge the lad's presence with a wry, distant smile. However, most of his attention is on tying his lace to his soccer boots so that he can pick up the soccer ball next to him and get back to his game.

I saw him. He lives in the bushes where it's dark.

Ben is now in the park alone except for a dinosaur. Only the dinosaur's head can be seen some distance from Ben. Bushes and small trees surround and obscure the greater part of its body; not too much detail is apparent except that it does not look completely real or familiar.

The Illustrator

With many picture books, the author is also the illustrator. The same person writes the words and draws the pictures. That was not so with this book. The author had to find an illustrator who could create the pictures he wanted. So he took the manuscript to an illustrator, to discuss the story.

"What sort of dinosaur is it?" asked the illustrator. "Can you find me some pictures of what these dinosaurs actually looked like? What does the boy look like? What sort of hair and face does he have? What does the park look like? How many pages will the book have?"

Some of the illustrator's first rough sketches.

There were many things the author had not explained in the manuscript. So many little details had to be considered. They talked about the boy and dinosaur so much that they seemed real. After a while, the author and the illustrator both felt they understood the story better.

"Okay, I'll get to work on it," said the illustrator. "I'll try some sketch plans and characters and get back to you when I have something done."

For several weeks the illustrator sketched different ideas. Ideas for the characters. Ideas for setting out the pages. Ideas for planning the whole book.

The illustrator took his sketches to the author to discuss them.

"The dinosaur is just as I had imagined," said the author, "but the boy isn't. Can we change his hair and face a bit?"

So the illustrator did some more sketches. He also prepared a sequence, or plan, for the whole book. This was important. Each picture had to follow the page before so that the story would make sense.

The illustrator's first page plan.

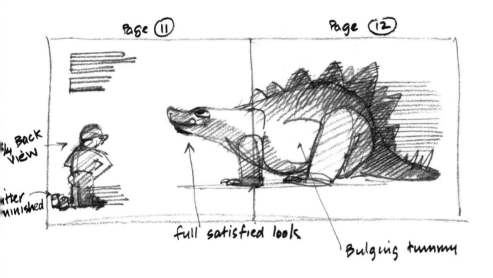

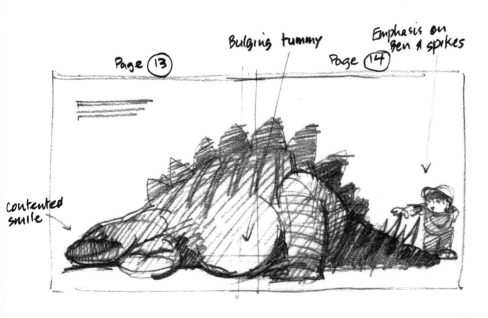

The illustrator had to decide on a style, or technique, to use in the book. Would he use paint, crayons, pencils, ink, or a mixture of these things to color the pictures? Would he use a brush, a pen, or a palette knife to put on the color? He began to experiment.

He tried pencil.

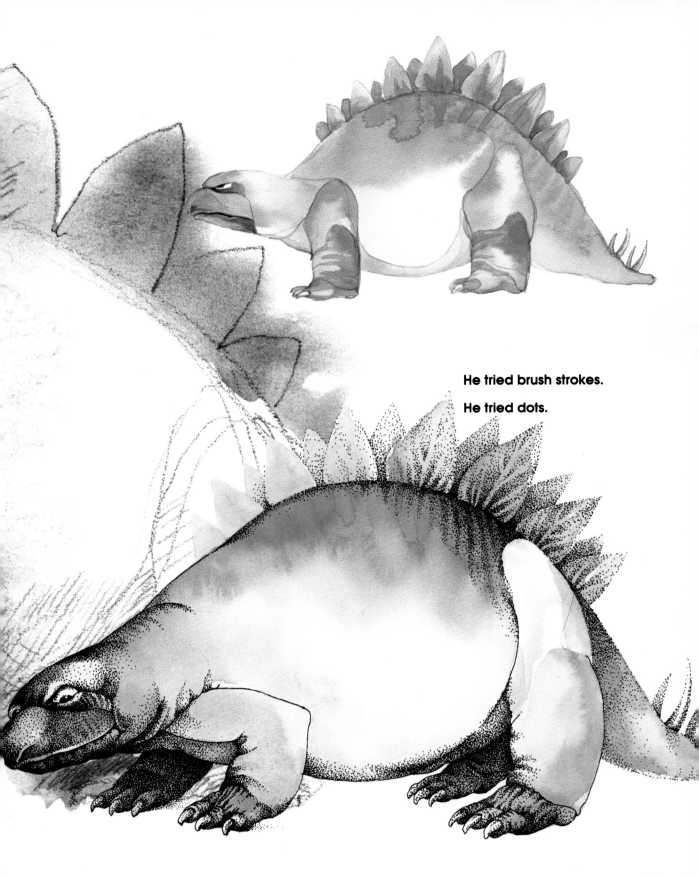

He tried brush strokes.

He tried dots.

And he tried lines
with pen and ink.

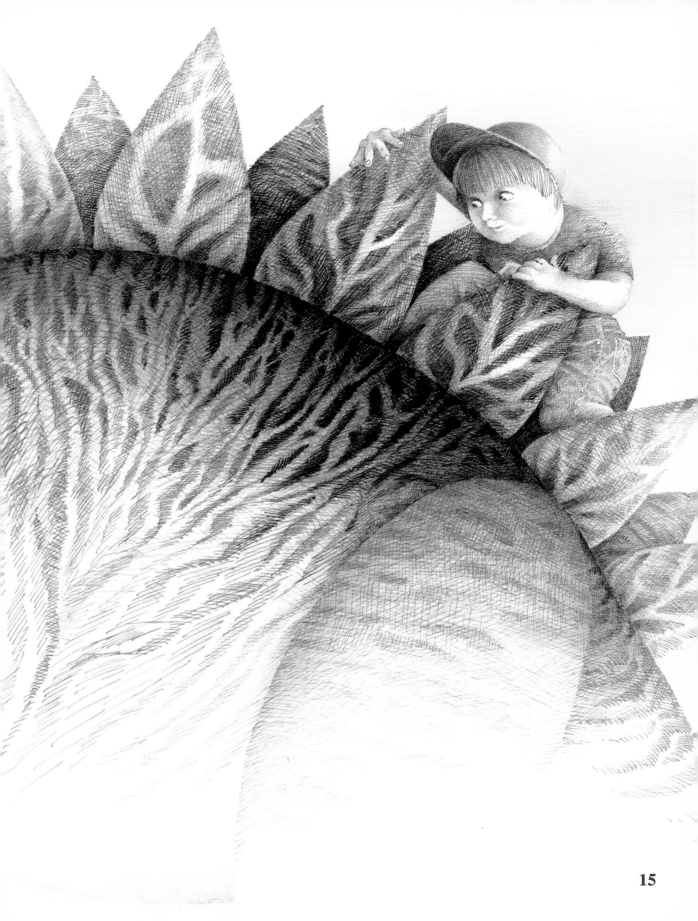

After discussing different sketches and techniques, the author and illustrator chose the one they preferred and changed details of the story, leaving out some pages and adding others.

The illustrator began the final artwork, which would take months because he had chosen a difficult style. The author went back to the word processor to make final changes to his text and to retype the manuscript, leaving double spaces between lines. The story was ready to take to the publisher.

The illustrator took many months to draw the pictures.

The publisher was the person who read the book to decide if it was the kind of book the company would like to publish. If the answer was yes, the publishing house would make all the arrangements to get the book edited, designed, made into film, printed, bound, and sold.

To get all this work done, many people at the publishing house would have to work with the book. To complete their tasks, they would need about four to five weeks.

The publisher talks with an editor.

THE EDITOR

The publisher called up one of the editors. An editor is someone who works with the text and who sometimes must ask the author to make changes. For instance, the author referred to a "drink can" that was thrown into the dinosaur's mouth. The editor might change that to "soda can" because "soda" seems the term children would more commonly use.

The publisher and editor looked at the manuscript and illustrations to decide if they wanted to publish the book.

"What do you think of this manuscript?" asked the publisher. "Is it worth risking money on?"

The editor read the story and thought about it. "I think this book is different," said the editor to the publisher. "It would probably sell well because children will like it."

"I thought so too," replied the publisher. "Let's do it."

One job of the editor was to notify the Library of Congress in Washington, DC, that the book was to be published. She gave the book a special number called an ISBN, which stands for *International Standard Book Number*. Then she sent the text of the book to the Library of Congress. They sent her the following information, to be placed in the book.

1. AUTHOR

2. TITLE OF BOOK

3. NAME OF BOOK SERIES

4. DESCRIPTION OF STORY

5. SUBJECT HEADINGS
(The book's title will be listed under these headings in library catalogs.)

6. ADDED ENTRIES
(The title will also appear under these headings in library catalogs.)

7. LIBRARY OF CONGRESS CLASSIFICATION NUMBER

8. LIBRARY OF CONGRESS CATALOG CARD NUMBER

9. ISBN
(The term "lib. bdg." refers to "library binding," a sturdy binding for books sold to schools and libraries.)

Library of Congress Cataloging-in-Publication Data

1. Martin, Rodney.
2.   There's a dinosaur in the park!

3.   (A Quality time book)
4.   Summary: A young boy's imagination brings to life a dinosaur playmate in the park.

5.   [1. Dinosaurs — Fiction. 2. Imagination — Fiction. 3. Play — Fiction] 6. I. Siow, John, ill. II. Title.

7. PZ7.M364184Th   1987 [E]   8. 86-42811

9.   ISBN 1-55532-151-8 (lib. bdg.)

After the manuscript was just right, the editor gave it to the designer, who then began to prepare the layout of the book. One job was to design the covers. Another was to choose the font — the style and size of type. It had to look right with the illustrations.

After the designer was finished, an editor checked the text again and returned it to the designer. The designer sent it to the typesetter along with written instructions about how to set up the type.

Instructions for the typesetter.

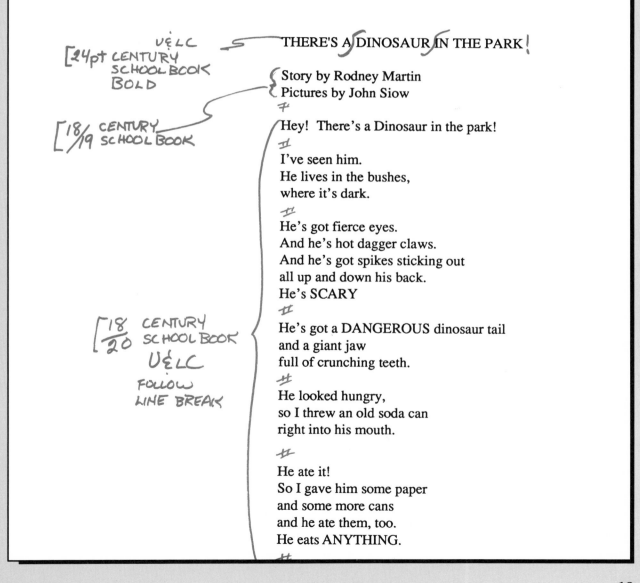

[24pt CENTURY SCHOOL BOOK BOLD — U&LC

THERE'S A DINOSAUR IN THE PARK!

Story by Rodney Martin
Pictures by John Siow

[18/19 CENTURY SCHOOL BOOK

Hey! There's a Dinosaur in the park!

I've seen him.
He lives in the bushes,
where it's dark.

He's got fierce eyes.
And he's hot dagger claws.
And he's got spikes sticking out
all up and down his back.
He's SCARY

He's got a DANGEROUS dinosaur tail
and a giant jaw
full of crunching teeth.

[18/20 CENTURY SCHOOL BOOK U&LC FOLLOW LINE BREAKS

He looked hungry,
so I threw an old soda can
right into his mouth.

He ate it!
So I gave him some paper
and some more cans
and he ate them, too.
He eats ANYTHING.

19

THE KEYLINER

The type came back from the typesetter. When it arrived, the keyliner, a person in the art department, cut it into sections and carefully placed it into position on large pieces of poster board. These are called the "boards," or the "keylines." The type was placed exactly as it would appear in the finished book, with margins carefully marked.

The type as it came from the typesetter.

THERE'S A DINOSAUR IN THE PARK
2/3/89 TYPE STYLE: CENTURY SCHOOLBOOK

Story by Rodney Martin
Pictures by John Siow

THERE'S A DINOSAUR IN THE PARK!

Hey! There's a Dinosaur in the park!

I've seen him.
He lives in the bushes,
where it's dark.

He's got fierce eyes.
And he's hot dagger claws.
And he's got spikes sticking out

The keyliner also placed photocopies of the illustrations on these boards. This, too, was done very carefully according to measurements the designer had decided upon when doing the layout.

The keyliner also prepared the covers in this way, placing both the illustration and type in just the right places.

The keyliner placed photocopies of the illustrations on the boards.

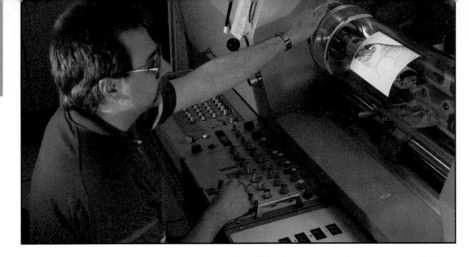

THE FILMHOUSE

The scanner, or separator, separated the illustration into four colors, one piece of film for each color.

The magenta, yellow, cyan, and black dots, enlarged.

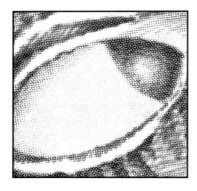

The technician checked the film to see that the text printed well on the black.

The illustrations were sent to the filmhouse, where a machine called a scanner electronically recorded one color at a time onto film, producing four different films for each drawing. The colors that it recorded were black, yellow, magenta (a kind of red), and cyan (a kind of blue). It also separated the pictures into dots so tiny they could hardly be seen. Of course, the machine did not damage the original drawings.

Soon the boards arrived, and the type on them was also photographed and made into film. The technician positioned this over the black film made earlier and created a new film combining them both.

Technicians used these four films to make a "color proof." They checked it to see that the color matched the color in the original illustrations. They also produced a mockup of the book called the bluelines, or "blues"; it gets its name from its pale blue color. Looking at the bluelines, the editors could check the type again, and the designer could be sure the pictures and type were positioned just right.

The production director works for the publisher. She schedules work at the filmhouse and the printing company and works with the art and editorial departments so that work is done on time. After the film was produced, she had to approve of the film before the printer could begin. She compared the color proofs to the original illustrations.

"No, they're not right," she said. "The color is off."
So the proofs went back to the filmhouse and the separator to be corrected.
"What a fussy person," thought the people at the filmhouse. Another set of proofs appeared.
"They're better," said the production director.
In the meantime, the editor and the designer examined the bluelines to see if everything would look right in the final book. The bluelines looked just fine.
"Okay," said the production director to the people at the filmhouse, "you can send the four films, the color proofs, and the bluelines to the printer."

The production director inspected color proofs.

THE PRINTER

The platemaker placed
the film over the top of
the plate.

Insets:
Film (upper) and
plate (lower).

At the printer's, the platemaker laid out the four films onto a metal plate and placed them into another machine. This machine exposed the film, and the image was transferred from the film onto thin sheets of metal. These sheets of metal are called the "printing plates." There were four different printing plates for each set of pages — one plate for yellow, one for magenta, one for cyan, and one for black.

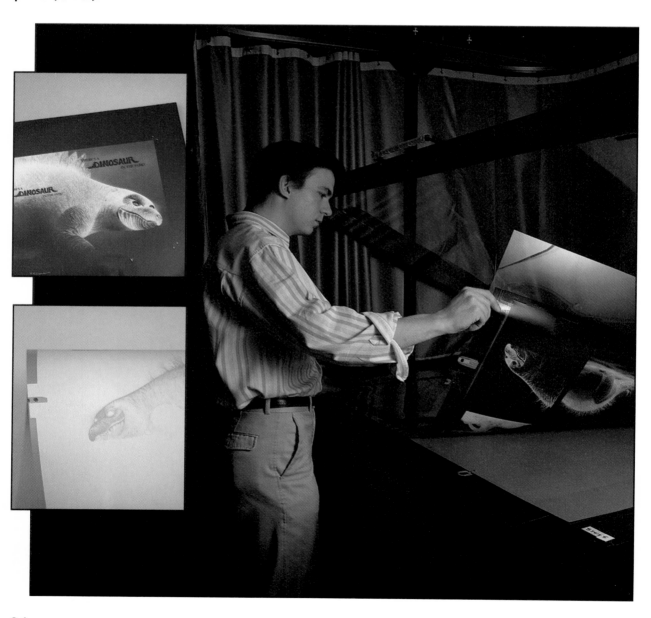

The press operator fit these plates onto the offset printing press, which transfers the image from the plate to a roller. The ink on the roller then transfers the image to the paper.

Large sheets of paper rolled through the press, picking up the four different-colored inks — yellow, magenta, cyan, and black. First the machine printed all the yellow parts of the pictures. Then it printed all the magenta on top of the yellow. Then the cyan sections, then the black.

As the machine printed the separate colors onto the paper, the fine dots overlaid one another to make other colors. Cyan dots and yellow dots merged to make green; magenta and yellow became orange, and so on.

When all four colors were printed, the pictures once again looked like the illustrator's original drawings. The words were printed when the black ink went on. Once again, the production director had to check the color in the book.

A technician again checked the color.

This offset press printed the four colors one at a time.

Although all the pages of the book had been printed, they were all on flat sheets of paper. Each book was one sheet with sixteen pages on each side. The pages seemed to be in odd positions; some were upside-down, and they all looked out of order. The book could not be read like that. It was like huge jigsaw pieces scattered over a large sheet of paper.

A sheet of printed pages, before it was folded.

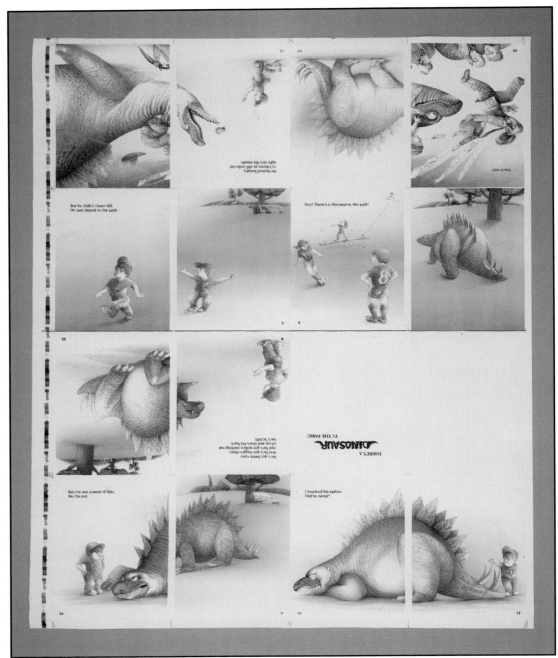

The printers then began the process of folding, stapling, stitching, and gluing the book together.

One at a time, the sheets of paper for the pages were fed into a folding machine. Each sheet was folded four times and finally ended up as 16 pages, with pictures on both sides, which made it a 32-page book. This folded section is called a "signature."

The printed sheets were folded into sections.

Inset: a signature.

Then a machine placed endpapers around the signature. This paper was heavier because it would be glued to cardboard to make a cover.

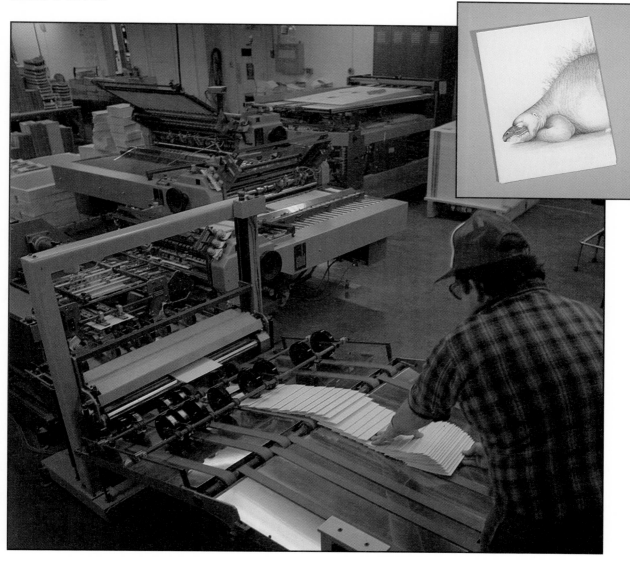

This signature was then stitched on a special sewing machine. Although the pages were then all in their correct order, you would still not be able to read the book because you would not be able to turn the pages. They were still joined at the edges where the sheets had been folded.

The sections were fed into a sewing machine.

Inset: a stitched but untrimmed book.

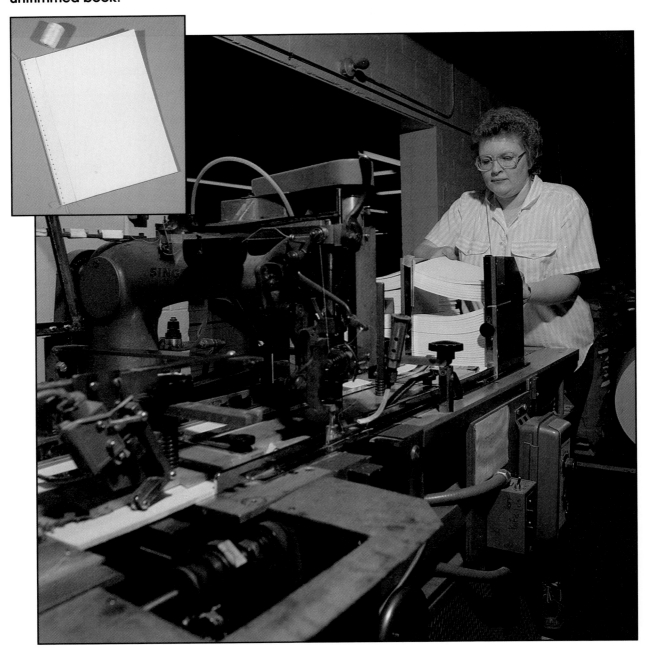

The pages were placed in a cutting machine that is called a "guillotine." The top, bottom, and edge (but not the side that was stitched) were trimmed just a bit so that the folds were cut off. The pages could then be opened because they were joined only at the spine (the back or stitched edge).

The pages were trimmed on a guillotine.

Inset: a stitched and trimmed book.

Upper: the case.

The pages were glued to the inside of the case.

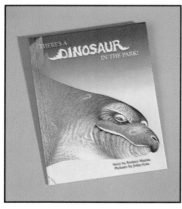

At last, the finished book!

The picture for the cover had been printed on separate pieces of paper. Sheets of this paper moved through a machine that applied glue to the back surface and pressed three pieces of cardboard onto the glue. Then it wrapped the cover around the edges of the cardboard, making what is called the "case."

Finally, the pages were fixed to the case. This was done by gluing the endpapers, the very first and the very last pages of the book, to the insides of the case. The book was then finished and ready to be delivered to the publisher.

Everyone involved in making the book was excited.
"Let's throw a party," said the publisher. "I'll pay."

So they had a party with librarians, booksellers, and friends. And the little boy and his dinosaur appeared on bookshelves all over the country.

There is only one other part to tell . . .

**WHAT HAPPENED TO
THE DINOSAUR IN THE PARK?**

. . . but that's another story.

Glossary

bluelines — Mockups of books prepared at the filmhouse so publishers may see what their book will look like after the printer assembles it.

boards — Sturdy poster board on which type and photocopies of illustrations are placed before being sent to the filmhouse.

case — The 3-piece cardboard covering of the book, with the cover illustration and endpapers glued to it.

color proof — Sample sheet prepared at the filmhouse so that the production director and designer can compare the color as it will appear in the book to the color in the original illustrations.

endpapers — Sturdy paper at the beginning and end of a book; it is glued to the book's cover.

font — A set of type of one size and face, or style.

guillotine — A machine that trims the edges of the folded sheets making up the book.

illustrations — Photographs or drawings used with text to help readers understand stories and other written material.

keylines — *See* **boards**.

Library of Congress — A U.S. institution based in Washington, D.C., that keeps a record of nearly every book published in the United States.

manuscript — The text that the author prepares.

plates — The metal plates used on the printing press to transfer the story and illustrations to paper.

scanner — *See* **separator**.

separator — A machine that separates the colors in an illustration into the four primary colors: yellow, cyan, magenta, and black.

signature — Sheet of paper printed on both sides which, when folded into 16 pages and then stitched and glued, makes up a 32-page book.

spine — The part of the book where the folded, uncut pages meet; the part that shows when a book is on a library shelf.

typesetter — A person or business that prepares the final type that will be filmed when a book is sent to the filmhouse.

word processor — A program that allows people to use their computers as they would a typewriter.

Index